FEB **2 6** 2008

BEES

Joyce James

Grolier
an imprint of

www.scholastic.com/librarypublishing

Published 2008 by Grolier
An imprint of Scholastic Library Publishing
Old Sherman Turnpike, Danbury,
Connecticut 06816

For The Brown Reference Group plc
Project Editor: Jolyon Goddard
Copy-editors: Lesley Ellis, Lisa Hughes,
    Wendy Horobin
Picture Researcher: Clare Newman
Designers: Jeni Child, Lynne Ross,
    Sarah Williams
Managing Editor: Bridget Giles

Volume ISBN-13: 978-0-7172-6217-5
Volume ISBN-10: 0-7172-6217-0

**Library of Congress
Cataloging-in-Publication Data**

Nature's children. Set 1.
    p. cm.
  Includes index.
  ISBN-13: 978-0-7172-8080-3
  ISBN-10: 0-7172-8080-2
  1. Animals--Encyclopedias, Juvenile.
  QL49.N38 2007
  590--dc22

                              2007018358

Printed and bound in China

PICTURE CREDITS

Front Cover: Shutterstock: Stefan
Glebowski.

Back Cover: Shutterstock: Ariel Bravy,
Christian Musat, Mark William Penny,
Florin Bravy.

Ardea: Jason Mason 33, Richard Becker 17;
Nature PL: John B. Nee 18, Premaphotos
46, Kim Taylor 42; **Photolibrary.com**: James
Robinson 21; **Shutterstock**: Maciek Barab
38, Miles Boyer 5, Borut Gorenjak 26–27,
Jasenka Luksa 10, Christian Musat 13,
Andrea Nantal 30, Mark William Penny 9,
Radu Rasvan 4, Rose Thompson 14, Florin
Tirlea 29, Van Truan 2–3, 6, 41, Joanna
Zopoth-Lipiejko 45, **Still Pictures**: Denis
Bringard 37, Hecker 34, K. Wothe 22.

Contents

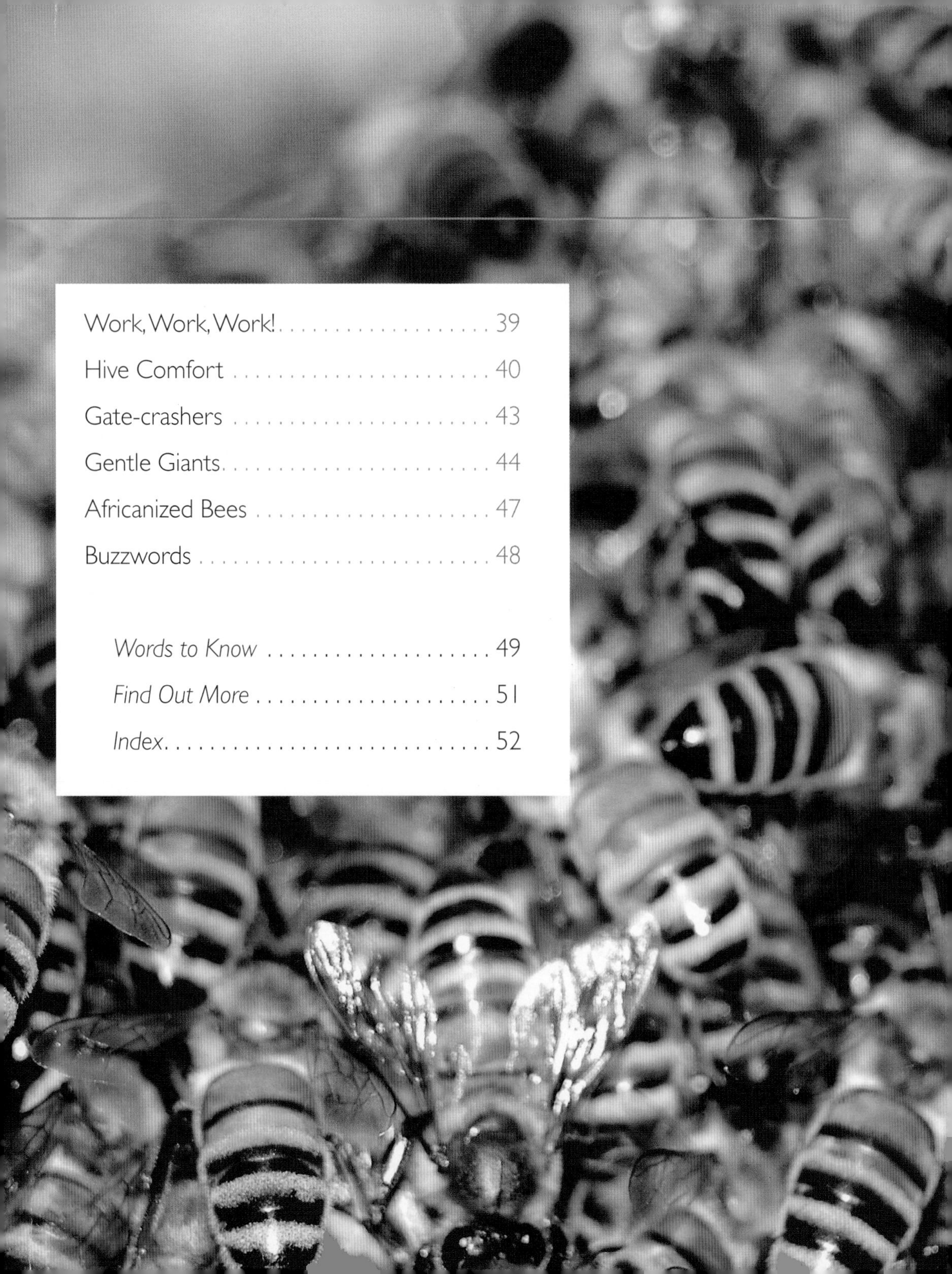

FACT FILE: Honeybees

Class	Insects (Insecta)
Order	Ants, bees, sawflies, and wasps (Hymenoptera)
Family	Long-tongued bees (Apidae)
Genus	Honeybees (*Apis*)
Species	Western honeybee (*Apis mellifera*)
World distribution	Honeybees occur naturally in Europe, Asia, and Africa; people have introduced them into North and South America and Australia
Habitat	Wherever there are flowers that make nectar
Distinctive physical characteristics	Furry abdomen with black and yellow stripes; six jointed legs; two pairs of wings; jointed feelers; large eyes; stinger at end of abdomen
Habits	Honeybees are social insects that live in large colonies; workers, drones, and the queen bee have different roles in the hive
Diet	Grubs eat pollen, honey, and royal jelly; adults drink nectar and eat honey

Introduction

Why have honeybees been friends to people for thousands of years? Because they produce **honey**, of course! Honey is a gooey, sweet substance that bees make and eat. It's packed with energy and keeps bees busy and buzzing. People like honey, too. Farming bees to collect their honey is called beekeeping. Beekeepers provide a wooden box—a beehive—for the bees to make their home. It's not just the bees' honey that people take. Honeybees make **beeswax**, too. People have many uses for beeswax, including shoe and furniture polish and candles. Beeswax is sometimes used as hair and mustache wax, too!

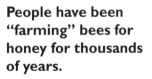

People have been "farming" bees for honey for thousands of years.

Honeybees are
social insects. They
live in a big group
called a colony.

A Lot of Bees

There are about 20 thousand types, or species, of bees. Only about 800 types of bees live in big groups, or colonies. The rest are solitary— they live alone. There are seven species of honeybees. Those include the dwarf honeybee, giant honeybee, and Himalayan honeybee. All honeybees produce beeswax and honey. Only the Western, or European, honeybees make large amounts of honey that can be collected by people. That is the bee you are most likely to see buzzing around in your backyard.

The Western honeybee occurs naturally in Europe, Asia, and Africa. In 1622, European settlers brought honeybees to America. The bees spread across America faster than the settlers. Honeybees are now also common in South America and Australia.

Bee Basics

Bees are insects. All insects have a body divided into three main parts: a head, thorax, and abdomen. The round head has mouthparts, enormous eyes, and **antennas**, or feelers. The thorax is the middle section. It bears three pairs of jointed legs and the wings. The abdomen is the biggest part. In honeybees, it is covered in hairs that form black and yellow bands. At the end of the abdomen there is a stinger.

The hairs on a bee's body keep the bee warm. That allows it to fly in weather too cold for most other insects. The hairs are also sensitive to touch and help the bees communicate in the darkness of the **hive**. Honeybees have a long flexible tongue. The tongue can move in any direction. It can also be stretched out to about the same length as the honeybee's head. The back pair of a honeybee's legs have baskets for collecting **pollen**.

When a honeybee
has filled its pollen
baskets, it heads
back to the hive.

A bee's two compound eyes allow it to see in almost all directions.

Big Eyes

Have you ever noticed a bee's huge eyes? The two eyes covering the sides of a bee's head are called compound eyes. They are made up of thousands of tiny parts. The tiny parts work together to build a picture of the bee's surroundings. Compound eyes are good for picking up movement. But they do not give bees the sharp vision that you have. Bees cannot see the color red but they can see the color ultraviolet. Humans cannot see that color. Many flowers that bees visit have ultraviolet petals or markings.

Bees also have three much smaller eyes on the top of the head. These eyes are called simple eyes. They do not see too well. They tell the bee the position of the Sun when the bee is outside the hive, looking for nectar and pollen.

Sensational Bees

A bee's antennas are often called feelers. They have many joints and point downward. The antennas not only feel. They have tiny hairs that smell and taste chemicals in the air. Scientists are currently using bees to detect explosives because their sense of smell is so good. There are hairs around the bee's mouth that can taste. And the hairs all over the body help "hear" sounds by picking up vibrations in the air.

Hairs can also detect changes in air pressure. This lets bees know when it is going to rain. Bees don't like rain! They stay in the hive on rainy days.

The antennas and the tiny
hairs that cover a bee's body
help the insect get a sense
of its surroundings.

A bee's delicate but powerful wings can beat so fast that they look like a blur.

Wonderful Wings

Bees belong to a group of insects called hymenopterans (HI-MUH-NOP-TUR-RUNS). That means "membrane wing." A membrane is a very thin, see-through film, like plastic wrap. Bees look like they have only one pair of wings. In fact bees have two pairs: A large pair of forewings and a smaller pair of hind wings. In flight, each hind wing is attached by little hooks to the forewing in front. The wings work together as a single unit on each side of the bee.

The wings do a lot of work. In flight they beat about 11,400 times a minute, or 190 times a second! The wings flap so fast that they look like a blur. You might think the buzz you hear comes from the wings. But the buzz is actually from the vibrating flight muscles inside the bee's thorax. Honeybees can fly as fast as 15 miles per hour (24 km/h). After about 15 minutes, however, the bees need to rest and feed to replenish their energy stores.

Keep Away: Stripes

The yellow and black stripes on a honeybee's body act as a warning that it can and will sting if threatened. If a predator has eaten a bee before and been stung, the predator remembers and will avoid bees in the future. Other stinging bees and wasps also have these markings.

Some clever insects without a stinger have copied bees. They have stripes, too. They include beeflies, hoverflies, and some moths. They depend on this copycat coloring to keep predators away.

Stings and stripes don't keep all predators away, however. Some birds, such as mockingbirds, eat bees. Skunks, raccoons, and opossums also enjoy a tasty snack of bees.

A beefly mimics a
honeybee's coloring
to keep predators away.

A worker stings a
human. The stinger
detaches from the
bee's body.

Bee-ware!

Workers usually use their stinger only once. If the worker stings, the stinger is likely to detach from the bee's body. If the stinger is detached, it usually takes organs along with it, killing the bee in the process. A worker honeybee's stinger has little barbs that become lodged in the victim. Muscles in the stinger pump out **venom**, or poison, and bury the stinger deeper into the victim.

Queen honeybees have a smoother stinger that they can remove easily from a victim. They can sting many times. They only sting to kill rival queens when fighting over who will be queen of the hive. Male honeybees, or **drones**, do not have a stinger.

Not all bees sting. Stingless bees are small and live mostly in hot, tropical places. Instead of stinging when threatened, they bite. Fire bees are a type of stingless bee with a fearsome bite. When they bite, they release chemicals that cause burning blisters.

Honeycomb Hives

Worker bees build a home out of beeswax. They build many compartments, or **cells**. Together these are called a **honeycomb**. Each cell is six sided, or hexagonal. In the wild, honeybees make their home, or nest, in a hole in a tree or in the ground. The honeycombs hang down from the roof of the hollow. Beekeepers provide a **colony** with its own sheltered space—a sturdy wooden box called a beehive.

Honeybees have a gland on the abdomen that produces the beeswax. The wax comes out as flakes. The worker bee then uses its mouthparts to chew and soften the flakes. The bee then adds the wax to the honeycomb to build new cells. The cells are used for storage—a bit like cupboards, shelves, and drawers in your kitchen. Cells might contain pollen, honey, eggs, **grubs**, or **pupae**. Worker bees produce wax a few days after becoming adults. They do so for about two weeks. After that, they are too old to make wax properly so they do other types of work.

Honeycombs, created by
worker bees, are made
up of expertly crafted
six-sided storage cells
constructed from wax.

21

The queen bee has a long, thin abdomen. Her life is spent laying eggs in the hive.

Inside the Hive

In a honeybee colony, there are three types, or castes, of honeybees. There is one adult queen, 100 or so male drones, and thousands of workers—up to 80,000 in a big colony.

The colony is like a castle. Workers guarding the entrance identify members of the same colony by their smell. Other workers go about their jobs in the hive, such as building cells or feeding grubs. At the heart of the colony is the queen. She lays eggs and is looked after by the workers, who are all her daughters. The queen is bigger than the other bees—about 0.9 inches (2.2 cm) long.

If the colony gets too large, the queen sends out scouts to find a place suitable for a new colony. She then lays eggs that will become new queens and leaves the hive. A swarm of 10,000 or so bees accompanies the queen. They set up a new nest. In the old hive, new queens soon hatch. One queen kills off all the others. The new queen then leaves the nest to mate with drones. She soon returns to lay eggs, and life in the hive returns to normal.

Nectar and Pollen

Bees make honey from nectar. Nectar is a sugary liquid made by certain flowers especially for bees. Why are flowers so helpful to bees? Well, they do expect something in return. The bees spread pollen from flower to flower. Pollen must be transferred from one flower to another to make seeds. Plants can't do that themselves because they can't move around. So bees help.

Many flowers have brightly colored petals and sweet scents that attract bees. The petals often have ultraviolet lines, or guides, that only the bee can see. These guides direct the bee to the nectar. While drinking the nectar, pollen brushes onto the bee's hairs. As the bee flits from flower to flower, it spreads pollen among the flowers. That is called pollination. It also makes bees very useful to fruit farmers.

Honey Stomach

Worker bees use their flexible tongue to remove nectar from flowers. Honeybees have powerful sucking muscles in their throat. They store the nectar in a special sac in their abdomen. The sac is called a **honey stomach**, or crop. It can expand greatly to contain a lot of nectar.

Honeybees also collect and eat pollen. Pollen contains many nutrients that are good for bees. Honeybees have their own "shopping baskets," called pollen baskets, attached to their hind legs. The bee uses bristles on its other legs to comb pollen into the baskets. When the pollen baskets are bulging to the brim, the worker returns to the hive. A food-finding honeybee visits between 50 and 1,000 flowers a day.

Only the older workers get to leave the hive to visit flowers.

Let's Dance

What is the first thing a worker does after returning to the hive with a belly full of nectar and full pollen baskets? It does a dance! The dance tells other workers where to go to find the nectar and pollen.

Workers gather around the dancer and follow the bee's movements with their antennas. The dancing bee runs around in tight figure-eights and shakes, or waggles, its abdomen. That tells the other food-collecting bees the direction of and the distance to the flowers. Other bees then make a beeline for the flowers.

Bees returning to the hive cough up, or regurgitate, partly digested nectar into cells. Water in the nectar evaporates, or turns to gas. That thickens the nectar, turning it into honey. Sometimes, workers flap their wings over the liquid to quicken the honey-making process. When a cell is full of honey, it is sealed, or capped, with beeswax.

Bees tell other bees in the hive where flowers are by dancing.

Once a cell is full of honey, workers seal it. This stored honey is eaten during winter.

Healthy Honey

A single honeybee makes about a twelfth of a teaspoon of honey in its lifetime. One pound (0.45 kg) of honey—that's about the same as a big jar you can buy in the supermarket—is made from the nectar of about two million flowers!

What do bees need honey for? Like you, they eat it to get energy. Honey even contains substances that can kill disease-causing germs. Honey mixed with pollen is called "**bee bread**." Grubs that become workers and drones eat bee bread for three days before they become pupae. Adult bees survive on honey over the winter when it's too cold for bees to leave the hive. A large colony might eat as much as 44 pounds (20 kg) of honey over winter.

Growing Up

As you grow, you look pretty much the same. Bees, on the other hand, have four life stages. At each life stage the bee looks completely different. Those life stages are egg, larva (grub), pupa, and adult.

A bee's egg is the size of a pinhead. Only the queen lays eggs. She lays eggs inside cells called brood cells. After about three days the egg hatches and out wriggles a tiny white wormlike grub.

Worker nurses feed the young grubs on a creamy substance called **royal jelly** for the first few days. Royal jelly is made by glands in the nurses' head. The jelly contains a lot of nutrients. If a grub is fed nothing but royal jelly the grub eventually becomes a queen. If a grub's food is switched to bee bread, the young bee becomes a worker or a drone.

After six days, the grub becomes a pupa. In this stage, the grub stops wriggling and eating. It spins a hard case called a **cocoon**. Inside the cocoon the pupa changes from a grub into a winged adult.

Bee grubs stay in their cell. They are fed more than 1,000 times a day by worker bees!

A bumblebee emerges from its cocoon.

Emerging Adults

When a grub becomes a pupa, nurse workers seal the brood cell with beeswax. The time that each bee spends as a pupa depends on the type of bee it will become. Workers spend about 21 days as a pupa. Drones and queens spend a few days longer. When the worker bees emerge, they begin their chores. When the drones emerge, they fly off to find a queen to mate with.

But when queens emerge, it's war! They sting to death other emerging queens until one winner remains. She leaves the colony and finds drones to mate with. After that, the queen returns to the hive to lay about 1,500 to 2,000 eggs each day for three to five years—that's millions of eggs! Bees only rear queens when the old queen is about to die or when the colony gets too big and the existing queen flies off to form a new colony.

Droning On

Drones are male bees. They do not collect nectar and pollen. They do not guard the hive. Their only role is to mate with the queen. Drones grow from eggs that the queen makes without mating. The eggs that a queen lays after mating with a drone only become females—workers and a few queens. So drones do not have fathers or sons!

Drones are larger than workers, about 0.8 inches (2 cm) long. Males have bigger eyes and a stockier body. Their tongue is shorter. They die after mating. Those that do not get a chance to mate soon die, too. When the new queen has mated, the drones are no longer welcome in the hive. Their tongue is so short that they cannot feed themselves and soon starve to death.

Drones have no role in the hive. They can't even feed themselves—workers feed them.

This bee has left the hive to collect nectar and pollen.

Work, Work, Work!

Workers are the smallest bees in the beehive at about 0.6 inches (1.6 cm) long. They are all daughters of the queen. But unlike their queen mother, workers cannot lay eggs. Workers are there to work. They might have several different jobs in their lifetime, including hive builder, nurse, janitor, security guard, and food finder.

Most young worker bees make beeswax, look after the queen, and take care of the grubs. As they get a little older, they help unload and store food. The oldest workers have the most dangerous job. They are allowed out to collect nectar and pollen. Outside, they are at risk from bee-eating predators, such as mockingbirds. Workers that emerge in spring and summer often live about six weeks. Those workers that emerge later in the year survive winter, and live much longer.

Hive Comfort

Unlike birds and mammals, bees cannot control their body temperature. When it is cold, bees are sluggish and find it difficult to fly. That's why you don't see bees buzzing around in winter. But bees manage to keep their hive nice and warm during these cold months. How do they do that? They cluster and shiver. The heat that the bees give off raises the temperature inside the hive. They try to raise the temperature to an ideal 93.5°F (34°C).

But what if it gets too hot in the hive? Worker bees around the hive's entrance flap their wings. That draws cool air into the hive. Some workers might suck up water and squirt it around the hive to cool things down, too.

Bees raise the temperature in the hive during winter by shivering. Their movement creates heat.

Carpenter bees
live in holes bored
in wood.

Gate-crashers

You might sometimes have unwanted guests in your house, such as mice, cockroaches, and dust mites. Bee nests often have the same problem. Mites are tiny relatives of spiders. Sometimes, mites get into a hive and spread diseases that wipe out the whole colony.

However, mites are friends to some bees. Helpful mites eat trash in the hive! In a carpenter bees' nest tiny mites clean the grubs. The squeaky clean grubs are then less likely to catch certain diseases. The queen carpenter bee even has a special pouch for mites so she can take them to a new nest.

Cuckoo bees sneak into other bees' nests, lay eggs, and let worker bees raise the cuckoo bee grubs. Some moths also gate-crash hives and lay eggs. The moths' eggs hatch into grubs called caterpillars. These caterpillars, luckily, eat beeswax!

Gentle Giants

Bumblebees are big, hairy bees. Many are black, often with yellow, orange, or red bands of hair. Bumblebees are more easy going than many other types of bees. But these giants can still sting and can do so again and again.

Bumblebees live in colder places than other bees. Fuzzy hair and shivering warms them up. They are often the first bees we see in the spring. Bumblebees buzz around, pollinating early flowers such as bluebells. Like honeybees, bumblebees feed on nectar and collect pollen to feed their grubs.

Bumblebees live in small colonies, with a maximum of 200 bees. They build a nest in tunnels under the ground or in clumps of grass. Most bumblebee nests last less than a year because only the queen survives winter. The queen mates with drones in fall. She then leaves the nest to find a sheltered place to spend winter. In spring the queen emerges and lays eggs. Those eggs hatch into grubs that become the workers and drones for that year.

Bumblebees live in much smaller colonies than honeybees.

A swarm of Africanized bees has found a new place to build a nest.

Africanized Bees

In recent years, a type of honeybee called the Africanized bee has spread across South America and up into North America. This bee is a cross between a Western honeybee and an African honeybee. Africanized bees first appeared in 1957. Then, someone accidentally released some African queen bees into the wild in Brazil. These queens mated with honeybee drones. Their offspring spread rapidly.

Africanized bees look almost identical to Western honeybees. But they are far more defensive. If threatened, they are more likely to swarm and chase the intruder for a longer distance. Alarmed bees spread chemicals that tell other members of the hive to sting. The Africanized bee's venom isn't any stronger than that of the honeybee. Yet these bees are more likely to sting in large numbers. So they are more likely to hurt or even kill people. For this reason, Africanized bees are sometimes called "killer bees."

Buzzwords

Do you know anyone named Melissa or Deborah? *Melissa* comes from the Greek word and *Deborah* from the Hebrew word for "bee." Because bees have been part of our culture for so long, many words and phrases to do with bees and honey have entered the language.

Honey is sweet, and so it is often likened to pleasurable things. People often call someone they like "Honey." The early part of a marriage is called a honeymoon. If someone has a pleasant voice it is said to sound like oozing honey.

People working hard together might be called a "hive of activity." We make a "beeline" for something we want, like bees flying in a straight path to flowers. If you've got a "bee in your bonnet" you are thinking a lot about just one thing. That's a bit like a worker bee going about its job. And if you are well liked—you are "the bee's knees!" After reading this book, you might now think that bees themselves are the bee's knees!

Words to Know

Antennas   A pair of sensitive feelers on the bee's head used to smell and feel.

Bee bread   A mixture of honey and pollen fed to worker grubs.

Beeswax   An oily solid substance made by bees and used to make honeycomb.

Cells   Six-sided wax rooms that contain honey, pollen, grubs, or pupae.

Cocoon   A silky covering that a bee grub spins around itself when it pupates.

Colony   A group of bees that live and work together in a hive or nest.

Drones   Male bees.

Grubs   White wormlike and wingless baby bees. Also called larvae.

Hive	A bee colony's home.
Honey	A sweet, gooey, thick liquid made by bees from nectar. Bees eat honey.
Honeycomb	Beeswax cells in which honey and pollen are stored and eggs are laid.
Honey stomach	A part of a worker bee's gut where nectar is stored until the bee gets home.
Pollen	A sticky powder that flowers make and exchange to produce seeds.
Pupae	The life stage in which grubs turn into adults inside their cocoon.
Queen	The ruler of the bee colony.
Royal jelly	A special baby food for bee grubs.
Venom	Poison released from a bee's stinger.
Workers	Female bees who build the hive, tend the queen and grubs, and gather food.

Find Out More

Books

Dane Brimner, L. *Bees*. True Books–Animals. Danbury, Connecticut: Children's Press, 2000.

Green, E. K. *Bumblebees*. Blastoff! Readers. Eden Prairie Minnesota: Bellwether Media, 2006.

Web sites

Honey Bee
www.enchantedlearning.com/paint/subjects/insects/bee/Honeybeecoloring.shtml
Facts about honeybees and a picture to print and color in.

Honey Trivia
www.honey.com/consumers/kids/trivia.asp
A quiz to test your knowledge of honey.

Index